# THE 5 HUMAN
## *Sense's Success*

## (Rev.) George Paul Takyi

Ordering Information:

For orders and inquiries, please contact:
1-888-375-9818
www.toplinkpublishing.com
bookorder@toplinkpublishing.com

Printed in the United States of America

# THE 5 HUMAN
## *Sense's Success*

# CONTENTS

Dedication..................................................................................ix

Foreword..................................................................................xi

Introduction......................................................................... xiii

Chapter 1    The Sense of Sight (Seeing) Success............................1

Chapter 2    The Sense of "Hearing Success" ............................... 16

Chapter 3    The Sense of Tasting Success ...................................23

Chapter 4    The Sense of Smelling Success.................................29

Chapter 5    The Sense of Touching Success .................................34

Chapter 6    Creative Thinking.......................................................42

Conclusion ............................................................................... 53

Acknowledgement....................................................................63

About The Author ....................................................................65

About the Book.........................................................................67

Tribute to Aristotle rediscovery theory of the 5 Human Senses for the introduction of the book.

Tribute to the King James Version of the Bible. Copyright of Rev. Dr Morris Cerullo God's Victorious Army © 1996.

As all scripture verses are taken from the King James Version of the Bible.

Rev. George Paul Takyi
 (404-903-9112)
 (404-503-6780)
 U. S. A
 E-mail: takyiPaul1957@yahoo.com

Published By
Rev. George Paul Takyi
Printed in the United States of America (2016)

# DEDICATION

The builders of the house builds in vain without God the Father, the Son, and the Holy Spirit, this source of material could not have been fulfilled. That is why my profound gratitude goes to the Trinity for the breath of inspirational words of wisdom.

I also compliment my wife, Mrs. Helena Takyi, for solidly throwing her infringing support, and encouragement behind me as a wonderful source of motivation.

Together, we both achieve much as a team. And God bless us all for "Seeing" "Hearing" "Tasting" "Smelling" and "Touching" success.

# FOREWORD

Book writing comes out of philosophical and creative thinking by gathering of ideas together through determination and a dint of hard work to transforming vision into mission statements. So has the author communicated his ideas into writing this book.

I believe that every thousand mile begins with a step.

Therefore, it is not the best sellers, or authors who are the successful men and women in the market place. Because the race is not to the swift, nor the battle to the strong, neither yet bread to the wise, nor yet riches to the men of understanding, nor yet favour to men of skill: But time and chance happeneth to them all. (Eccl 9:11) KJV

Since "curiosity kills a cat", it is the key factor to read the book and judge it for yourself in order to give recognition to novice writers a chance to implement their God's given talents. I therefore implore all and sundry to get a copy of the five senses success to read, to locate their human resource potential.

Charles Boadi, (BEd, MBA, PhD Student) U.K.

# INTRODUCTION

## Why did I write this book?

The purpose for this write up "The five human sense's success is that everything God created in this universe was for a purpose, and a plan to conform its fitting especially for people created in the image and the likeness of God to use creative thinking to manipulate success as God's agents of creativity on earth.

I realized that great people are buried with their gifts, talents, skills, and competences in the graves without being remembered, or to let people know of their buried ideological, and philosophical experiences. If they had the chance to put their ideas into any shape or form of communication, in either audio, or visual material, though they are dead yet their rich experiences could benefit the living.

The bible says the dead cannot praise the Lord.

By reasoning, I decided to add value to the five basic principles of human sense's to success. Because, our gifts are the potential to elevate you to the higher heights. Failure to release our gifts leads to not finding our heavenly place in the world supermarket.

We therefore need to prepare for success and a thirst for it because great revivals were pursued fervently as the disciples of Jesus waited in the upper room for the outpouring of the Holy Spirit on the day of Pentecost at Jerusalem.

We need to pursue for success and not to relax into thinking that it is a destiny and heredity for the only few minority.

We need to work towards success, strategize for success and believe that though it lingers it will surely come.

"And the Lord answered me, and said, write the vision, and make it plain upon tables, that he may run that readeth it.

For the vision is yet for an appointed time, but at the end it shall speak, and not lie, though it tarry, wait for it: because it will surely come, it will not tarry (Habakkuk 2: 2-3) KJV.

God's word admonishes us that though, your success lingers it will surely come to pass.

For clarity of understanding the context of my book well, I chose to use the five basics of human senses by Aristotle, in order not to go into details about different theories from scholars, as some believe that human senses are more than five. Though, I don't dispute that fact but for the sake of simplicity. From theoretical point of research. Human have a lot more than five senses.

It turns out, that there are at least nine senses and most researchers think there are more like twenty one or so.

Just for reference, the commonly held definition of a "sense" is any system that consists of a group of sensory cell types that respond to a specific physical phenomenon and that correspond to a particular group of regions within the brain where the signals are received and interpreted.

According to Aristotle, the commonly held senses are as follows:-

1. "Seeing" <u>Sight</u>, this is technically two senses in the nod shed given the two distinct types of receptors present, one for color [cones] and one for brightness [rods].

2. "Tasting" <u>Taste</u>, this is sometimes argued to be five senses by itself due to the differing types of taste receptors [sweet, salty, sour, bitter and umami], but generally is just referred to as one sense.

   For most of us who don't know, umami receptors detect the amino acid glutamate, which is a taste generally found in meat and some artificial flavoring. The taste sense, unlike sight, it is a sense based off of a chemical reaction.

3. "Touching" <u>Touch</u>, this has been found to be distinct from pressure, temperature, pain, and even itch sensors.
   - Pressure – Obvious sense is obvious
   - Itch: Surprisingly, this is a distinct sensor system from other touch related senses.
   - Thermoception: The ability to sense heat and cold. This also is thought of as more than one sense. This is not just because of the two hot/cold receptors, but also because there is a completely different type thermoceptor, in terms of the mechanism for detection, in the brain are used for monitoring internal body temperature.

4. "Sound" – Detecting vibrations along some medium, such as air or water that is in contact with your ear drums.

5. "Smelling" <u>Smell</u>: - Another of the sensors that work off of a chemical reaction.

   This sense combines with taste to produce flavors.

   - Proprioception: This sense gives you the ability to tell where your body parts are, relative to other body parts.

This sense is one of things police officers test when they pull over someone who they think is driving drunk.

The "close your eyes, and touch your nose" test is testing this sense etc. etc.

Some possible hints about a "woman who lost the ability to smell, taste, see, and hear" as a child was the first deaf-blind person to be fully educated. Stories like how the blind dream? And many other relevant stories.

As time will not permit me to go into details about the theories surrounding the aspect of whether human senses are five, or more than that. Therefore, the traditional five human senses as quoted by Aristotle, is the motivative and illustrative ways I have built ideas for success.

# CHAPTER ONE

# The Sense of Sight (Seeing) Success

Seeing, - sight, is a gift from God for the people of this world to see the beautiful things God created far and near in the universe, to give praise and adoration, to show our appreciations for what God has done for mankind.

This chapter deals importantly about man's ability to see success through the eye-gate pleasure. This world's life journey of success and failures depends on how far people can see things ahead of other people. The way people see and look into things affects their thinking habits. Some people are both physical and spiritually myopic which has affected their lives and made them into thinking that prosperity, or poverty was a destiny they inherited from their ancestors of which nothing could be done about it for survival. Before we can best understand what success is, and how we can be able to apply it to the five human senses, let us take the Bible point of view into consideration.

In the book of Joshua, and after the death of Moses, God charged Joshua, the assistant of Moses, to take charge and lead the children of Israel, to the Promised Land with the following conditions to succeed. Let us read the passage in its context. "Now after the death of Moses the servant of the Lord it came to pass, that the Lord spoke unto Joshua the son of Nun, Moses minister, saying, Moses my servant is dead: now therefore arise, go over this Jordan, thou, and all this people, unto the land which I do give to them, even to the children of Israel. Every place that the sole of your foot shall tread upon, that have I given unto you, as I said unto Moses, from the wilderness and this Lebanon even unto the great river, the river Euphrates, all the land of the Hittites, and unto the great sea toward the going down of the sun, shall be your coast.

There shall not any man be able to stand before thee all the days of thy life: as I was with Moses, so I will be with thee: I will not fail thee, nor forsake thee.

Be strong and of good courage: For unto this people shall thou divide for an inheritance the land, which I swore unto their fathers to give them.

Only be thou strong and very courageous, that thou mayest observe to do according to all the law, which Moses my servant commanded thee: turn not from it to the right hand or to the left, that thou mayest prosper withsoever thou goest. This book of the law shall not depart out of thy mouth: but thou shalt meditate therein day and night, that thou mayest observe to do according to all that is written therein: For then thou shall make thy way prosperous, and then thou shalt have a good success" (Joshua 1:1-8) KJV.

So success is an achievement of one's goal. It means that how far you see, and confront success is the height one can reach. Your attitude will determine the altitude.

Here is another story as God charged Moses to choose some men to go and explore the land of Canaan, where they were about to take possession from the children of Anak, to inherit the promised land of their fathers. They were to go and spy, view, see the land of promise, to taste the fruits of the land and bring a feedback report to their fellow brothers.

And as they went, and came back to their brothers they brought a negative report to Moses depending on what they saw which affected their success. But according to Joshua, and Caleb, men of good spirit, with good eye sights, saw the land as a prosperous land to possess it. They didn't see the giants, they didn't see the children of Anak, but they saw the Lord who was ahead of them to deliver and conquer. You see, the majority of the people saw challenges, and the giants as hindrance to their success. Let us read from the Bible.

"And Moses sent them to spy out the land of Canaan, and said unto them, get you up, this way southward and go up into the mountain:

And see the land, what it is, and the people that dwelleth therein, whether they be strong or weak, few or many:

Vrs 19  And what the land is that they dwell in, whether it be good or bad: and what cities they be that they dwell in, whether in tents, or in strongholds.

Vrs 20  And what the land is, whether it be fat or lean, whether there be wood therein or not, and be ye of good courage, and bring of the fruit of the land, now the time was the time of the first ripe grapes. (Num 13:17-20) KJV.

Vrs 23  "And they came unto the brook of EshCol, and cut down from thence a branch with one cluster of grapes, and they bare it between two upon a staff; and they brought of the pomegranates and of the figs.

Vrs 25  "And they returned from searching of the land after forty days. How did they search about the land? It was by looking around to see the environmental and the geographical setting of the land, its beauty, its fertile crescent to grow good cash crops to sustain the people. Yet they brought back evil report from the good land.

You see, in the microscopic eyes of some people are very bad to the extent that they only see one, other's see two, and some few see three. Let us learn a lesson from the majority negativity which retarded their success, had it not being Joshua, and Caleb, who saw three ahead of them to deliver God the Father, God the Son, and God the Holy Spirit. Oh what a wonderous works of the Trinity. All of them would have been consumed by the Lords anger.

Vrs 26   "And they went and came to Moses, and to Aaron, and to all the congregation of the children of Israel, unto the wilderness of Paran, to Kadesh: and brought back word unto them, and unto all the congregation and showed them the fruit of the land

Vrs 27   "And they told him and said, we came unto the land whither thou sentest us, and surely it floweth with milk and honey, and this is the fruit of it.

Vrs 28   "Nevertheless the people be strong that dwell in the land, and the cities are walled, and very great: and moreover we saw the children of Anak there.

Vrs 29   The Amalekites dwell in the land of the south, and the Hittites, and the Jebusites, and the Amorites, dwell in the mountains, and the Canaanites dwell by the sea, and by the Coast of Jordan.

Vrs 30   And Caleb stilled the people before Moses, and said, let us go up at once and possess it. For we are well able to overcome it.

Vrs 31   But the men that went up with him said, we be not able to go up against the people, for they are stronger than we.

Vrs 32   And they brought up an evil report of the land which they had searched unto the children of Israel, saying,
The land, through which we have gone to search it, it is a land that eateth up the inhabitants thereof: and all the people that we saw in it are men of great stature.

Vrs 33   And there we saw the giants, the sons of Anak, which come of the giant: and we were in our own sight as grasshoppers, and so we were in their sight" (Num 13,) KJV.

So, were they blind, to see the Amalekites, Hittites, the Jebusites, and the Amorites, who dwelt on the mountain, the Canaanites who dwelt by the sea, and by the Coast of Jordan?

The story here depicts sense of sight. Seeing things around us portrays an indefatigable fact that we can see success, ahead for a bright future, or failure of seeing giants for lack of faith and determination to conquer. That is the reason why people need to pursue success by working towards the confines of our God's given gifts, and talents. Let me recount on the story of Moses and the Israelites where success was displayed during their encounter with Pharaoh, and his charioteers at the Red Sea.

Exodus chapter fourteen, when the Israelites were encamped before Pi-hahiroth, between Migdol, and the sea, over against Baal-Zephon, the Egyptians pursued after them, all the horses and the chariots of Pharaoh, and his horsemen, and his army, and overtook them encamping by the sea, beside Pi-hahiroth, before Baal-Zephon.

Vrs 10    And when Pharaoh drew nigh, the children of Israel lifted up their eyes, and behold, the Egyptians marched after them: and they were sore afraid: and cried out unto the Lord.

The level of what we see around us, what we think about things, and what we believe, will determine our success or failure.

Vrs 11    And they said unto Moses, because there were no graves in Egypt, hast thou taken us away to die in the wilderness? Wherefore hast thou dealt thus with us, to carry us forth out of Egypt? Let us continue from verse – 13

"And Moses said unto the people, fear ye not, stand still, and "see" the salvation of the Lord, which he will shew to you today: for the Egyptians whom ye have seen today, ye shall see them again no more forever.

Vrs 14  The Lord shall fight for you, and ye shall hold your peace.

Vrs 15  And the Lord said unto Moses, wherefore criest thou unto me? Speak unto the children of Israel, that they go forward:

Vrs 16  But lift thou up thou rod, and stretch out thine hand over the sea, and divide it: and the children of Israel shall go on dry ground through the midst of the sea.

Vrs 17  And I, behold, I will harden the hearts of the Egyptians, and they shall follow them: and i will get me honour upon Pharaoh, and upon his horsemen.

Vrs 18  And the Egyptians shall know that I am the Lord, when I have gotten me honour upon Pharaoh, upon his chariot, and upon his horsemen.

Vrs 19  And the angel of God, which went before the camp of Israel, removed and went behind them. Hallelujah!

Vrs 20  And it came between the camp of the Egyptians, and the camp of Israel: and it was a cloud and darkness to them, but it gave light by night to these: So that the one came not near the other all the night.

Vrs 21  And Moses stretch out his hand over the sea: and the Lord caused the sea to go back by a strong east wind all that night, and made the sea dry land ,and the waters were divided.

Vrs 22  And the children of Israel went into the midst of the sea upon the dry ground: and the waters were a wall unto them on their right hand, and on their left.

<u>Vrs 23</u>  And the Egyptians pursued, and went in after them to the midst of the sea even all Pharaoh's horses, his chariots, and his horsemen.

<u>Vrs 24</u>  And it came to pass, that in the morning watch the Lord looked unto the host of the Egyptians through the pillar of fire and of the cloud, and troubled the host of the Egyptians.

<u>Vrs 25</u>  And took off their chariot wheels, that they drave them heavily So that the Egyptians said, let us flee from the face of Israel: For the Lord fighteth for them against the Egyptians.

<u>Vrs 26</u>  And the Lord said unto Moses, stretch out thine hand over the sea, that the waters may come again upon the Egyptians, upon their chariots, and upon their horsemen. Isn't that wonderful?

<u>Vrs 27</u>  And Moses stretched forth his hand over the sea, and the sea returned to his strength when the morning appeared: and the Egyptians fled against it: and the Lord overthrew the Egyptians in the midst of the sea.

<u>Vrs 28</u>  And the waters returned, and covered the chariots, and the horsemen, and all the host of Pharaoh that came into the sea after them: there remained not so much as one of them.

<u>Vrs 29</u>  But the children of Israel walked upon dry land in the midst of the sea: and the waters were a wall unto them on their right hand, and on their left. And finally, in verse 30 "Thus the Lord saved Israel that day out of the hand of the Egyptians: and Israel saw the Egyptians dead upon the seashore.

<u>Vrs 31</u>  And Israel saw that great work which the Lord did upon the Egyptians: and the people feared the Lord, and believed the Lord, and his servant Moses "so, Moses saw God's power to deliver. God's glory to bring fame, and his deliverance in the midst of the enemy. And the Red Sea, he saw success than nobody amongst the children of Israel saw. Moses, saw God ahead of the people, he saw the Israelites crossing the Red Sea in advance, yet the people were wavering in between. So here are some few examples of success through a sense of "sight" (seeing) though, we walk by faith, not by sight, does not contradict to seeing things around us to build or destroy our success. So the sense of "sight" (seeing) has two dimensions the physical sight, and the spiritual sight.

The physical dimension of sight is what has been explained above through Moses, the Israelites, Pharaoh, the Egyptians, and the Red Sea.

Joshua, Caleb, and the Israelites journey to spy the promised land, and other stories. The spiritual dimension for sight: could best be understood by Apostle Paul's letter to the church at Corinthians. He wrote this:-

"But if our gospel be hid, it is hid to them that are lost: in whom the god of this world hath blinded the minds of them which believe not, lest the light of the glorious gospel of Christ, who is the image of God. Should shine unto them" (2 Corinthians 4:3-4) KJV.

So seeing things in the spiritual dimension depicts of believing, and seeing things to materialize in the physical realm. Because, both physical, and spiritual blindness is a curse of being deprived of one's success. Unless people see it as a challenge to move from status-quo to develop their potential no matter how they are.

Sometimes, we need to see things happen before we could be motivated to do certain things, and at certain times, we don't need to see things happened in order for us to be motivated. Here is another experience in the Bible from Apostle Paul, and Silas, they saw God out of a praise at Caesarea, prisons when they were jailed for casting out demonic spirit of divination from a damsel.

In this situation, they needed not to see things from the physical, but from the spiritual perspective to build their faith on.

The bible says, at midnight, Paul and Silas, prayed, and sang praises unto God: and the prisoners heard them" And suddenly, there was a great earthquake, so that the foundations of the prison were shaken: and immediately all the doors were opened, and every one's bands were loosed.

And the keeper of the prison awakening out of his sleep, and seeing the prison doors open, he drew out his sword, and would have killed himself, supposing that the prisoners had been fled." But Paul cried with a loud voice, saying. Do thyself no harm: for we are all here. Then he called for a light, and sprang in, and came trembling, and fell down before Paul and Silas.

And brought them out, and said, sirs, what must I do to be saved? And they said, Believe on the Lord Jesus Christ, and thou shall be saved, and thou house " Acts 16:25-31. ( KJV ). So the scriptures above explains that Paul and Silas saw God in the circumstance of praise and they were delivered from prison.

What do we do when people goes into situations like this? This reminds me of my evangelistic journey to Burkina Faso in 1986, and how the Lord came to my rescue. Around 9:00pm after I had crossed the Black Volta by some Canoe men there was no vehicle to convey me to the next village. So I had to walk for about 20 miles to the next village called "Kumbo", and along the journey I even didn't know where I was heading towards. So I lit my torch light, and stopped after I had travelled for about 10 miles, I reached a cross-road not knowing which direction to go, I dropped and started praying to God for a direction. It was around 12:00 midnight, and when I was praying, I heard a voice of people coming ahead of me, and as they got closer to me, they asked me where I was going.

I told them of where I was going to, and they told me to give them my bag to carry and lead me to where I was going.

We walked for about 10 miles in the middle of the night to a nearby village about half a mile ahead and they gave me my bag and told me to go and stay there to have my rest. Until after one week in that village then shall I be able to wait for a vehicle to take me to my final destination, Lorbi, Gao, under "Bobo Duraso".

When I picked my bag from the three men, I was turning back to show my appreciation for their kind gesture. And you know what happened? I didn't see them again. And there the Lord spoke to me that they were not ordinary men but his ministering angels were sent to strengthen me for the journey he the Lord had sent me. Halleluiah! And for years in my ministry this divine visitation of the Lord is always felt more especially, anytime I face challenges in my ministry it strengthens me.

And for the three months I spent in Burkina-Faso, the Lord did signs and wonders very tremendously and even up to today, for the obedience I did to His call. So with the spiritual sight, we can see challenges as they confront us to be more than conquerors through him who loved us more than what we can think about.

Hebrews (chapter 11:1) reads that "Now faith is the substance of things hoped for the evidence of things not seen.

Vrs 2    For by it the elders obtained a good report.

Vrs 3    Through faith we understand that the world's were framed by the word of God, so that things which are seen were not made of things which do appear

Vrs 4    By faith Abel offered unto God a more excellent sacrifice than Cain by which he obtained witness that he was righteous, God testifying of his gifts: and by it he being dead yet speaketh.

Vrs 5    By faith Enoch was translated that he should not see death: and was not found because God had translated him: For before his translation he had this testimony, that he pleased God.

Vrs 6    But without faith it is impossible to please him: For he that cometh to God must believe that he is, and that he is a rewarder of them that diligently seek him" (KJV)

So God is not pleased with people who die with their dreams without been dreamt.

They had failed God and mankind. To go on to cite the examples of heroes of faith in the book of Hebrews are all motivated scriptures to see success in our eyes vision from spiritual point of view is not a deviant to the physical seeing into things. We therefore need a physical eyes for physical things of nature, and spiritual eyes for spiritual things.

**Vrs 7** By faith Noah, being warned of God of things not seen as yet moved with fear, prepared an ark to the saving of his house: by the which he condemned the world, and became heir of the righteousness which is by faith.

**Vrs 23** By faith Moses, when he was born, was hid three months of his parents, because they saw he was a proper child: and they were not afraid of the Kings commandment:

**Vrs 24** By faith Moses, when he was come to years, refused to be called the son of Pharaoh's daughter:

**Vrs 25** Choosing rather to suffer affliction with the people of God, than to enjoy the pleasures of sin for a season.

**Vrs 26** Esteeming the reproach of Christ greater riches than the treasures in Egypt: for he had respect unto the recompence of the reward.

**Vrs 27** By faith he forsook Egypt, not fearing the wrath of the King: for he endured, as seeing him who is invisible

**Vrs 33** Who through faith subdued kingdoms, wrought righteousness, obtained promises, stopped the mouth of lions.

**Vrs 34** Quenched the violence of fire, escaped the edge of the sword, out of weakness were made strong, waxed valiant in fight, turned to flight the armies of the aliens." (KJV)

And finally, to succeed, you need to follow the examples of successful men and women.

To read articles about them, and learn about their life styles. The heathen King Nebuchadnezzar, saw four men in the fierry furnance when he threw Shadrach, Meshach, and Abed-nego, into the fire. Then Nebuchadnezzer the king was astonied, and rose up in haste, and spake, and said unto his counsellors, did not we cast three men bound into the midst of the fire? They answered and said unto the King, True O King (Daniel 3:24-25) KJV.

<u>Vrs 25</u>  He answered and said, lo, I see four men loose, walking in the midst of the fire, and they have no hurt: and the form of the fourth is like the Son of God.

To conclude this series, sense of sight, many demonstrations have been illustrated in order to develop our five senses to get the success we need in life.

So in the final analysis, your level of sight is what motivates you to manipulate success. This story means that some people see one, in life. And others see only two, and some other people see three.

But the few minorities see four in their eyes vision.

It is my earnest prayer that as you finish reading the book, you may be elevated from your slumber, and see your heavenly place of royalty before you set your priorities right to get something doing. By determination I want people to aim high and say that, with God everything is possible as you only endeavor plan well to do it, you can. If we believe and work hard towards our dreams.

# WORDS OF WISDOM

- Reasoning leads to innovation, and innovation leads to inventions. (By rediscovery of why - how - where - when and what? Results to reasoning.
- Wisdom is the key element to reasoning to succeed.
- Without innovative thinkers we all becomes nobody's (By cheap talks people says, nobody is nobody)
- Your actions and inactions can affect your self-esteem, and can affect the things you do in life
- You don't wait to change, for a change to change you.
- Your character is positive and motivated student
- Keep your goals in your wallet, and visualize yourself achieving them.
- A fool, is a fool, if even he owns the world bank.
- Excellence, doesn't mean perfection.
- If you want to change your outer world and experiences, you must begin – by looking at your thoughts, feelings, and believe in yourself.
- High achievers are more likely to credit their own hard work, ability, talent and persistence.
- Until you begin to think, nothing good happens to your destiny
- Until you find out reasons, you cannot find out answers.
- There is a difference between merely religious activities and the reality of things
- Until you are burdened for certain functions forget about the manifestations of such functions.
- You are the controller of your destiny.

- Drivers - pilots - and riders, carries their own safety in their hands as they drive or operates machines.
- You hold the keys to unlock the supernatural to affect the natural.
- By reasoning to create, and re-create, through innovation, and inventions, wisdom becomes truthful to the innovator.

Without considering to give the whole world as a gift to a fool everything becomes a waste.

So let us get wisdom and understanding because it is a principal thing. Some of the few words from the words of wisdom were quotes from my college rector, Professor Edward Ade.

(Rector of Oracle University - Santasi, Ghana).

# CHAPTER TWO

# The Sense of "Hearing Success"

In the book of Joel chapter one. God was admonishing the children of Israel through the Prophet Joel saying, "Hear this, ye old men, and give "ear" all ye inhabitants of the land, hath this been in your days, or even in the days of your fathers? (Joel 1: 2--4) KJV.

Vrs 3   Tell ye your children of it, and let your children tell their children, and their children another generation.

Vrs 4   That which the palmerworm hath left hath the locust eaten: and that which the locust hath left, hath the cankerworm eaten : and that which the cankerworm hath left hath the caterpillar eaten.

This means that Israel was sensing danger of God's wrath and judgment, for nothing was left over for their survival from their fig trees, meat offering was cut off from the house of the Lord. Which had rendered them in a state of impoverishment for their disobedience to God.

There was an invasion of the enemy ransacked everything they owned in the land.

The people of Israel who had onced seen Gods success, and now they were seeing it no more. They had to learn their lessons from what they were seeing, not right as a result of invasion and calamity from their enemies. And that was the reason why the prophet was admonishing them by saying, "Hear this and give ear to what they were seeing, and hearing.

And this is the ethymological basis, facts about the sense of hearing. So success and failure can be seen, and heard about in our communities, and surroundings.

The prophet of God was admonishing Israel to rise up from mediocrity of hardship and work very hard towards their success to escape God's judgment finger and the wrath of God. By a dint of hard work through fasting and prayer for a change for better.

Joel 1:6    For a nation is come up upon my land, strong, and without number, whose teeth are the teeth of a lion, and he hath the cheek teeth of a great lion.

Vrs 7    He hath laid my vine waste, and barked my fig tree: he hath made it clean bare, and cast it away, the branches thereof are made white.

Vrs 8    Lament like a virgin girded with sackcloth for the husband of her youth.

Vrs 9    The meat offering and the drink offering is cut off from the house of the Lord: the priests, the Lord's ministers, mourn

Vrs 10    The field is wasted, the land mourneth, for the corn is wasted: the new wine is dried up, the oil languished.

Vrs 13    Gird yourselves, and lament, ye priests howl, ye ministers of the altar: Come, lie all night in sackcloth, ye ministers of my God: for the meat offering and the drink offering is witholden from the house of your God.

Vrs 14    Sanctify ye a fast, call a solemn assembly gather the elders and all the inhabitants of the land into the house of the Lord your God, and cry unto the Lord.

Sometimes we see our churches, and nations collapsing as a result of Gods judgment for people not doing right in the sight of God. And as leaders we do nothing about it rather we maneuver our ways as if we are doing things right and the situation worsens. .

We have heard and seen what God did to our forefathers yet we don't care, the leaders are always concerned about win win situations more especially, the third- world nations leaders. Majority of them are very selfish to always amass wealth to themselves whilst the majority of the people are suffering.

May God give us the spiritual eye sight and understanding to the Prophet Habakkuk's prayer. He said, "O Lord, I have heard thy speech, and was afraid: O Lord, revive thy work in the midst of the years, in the midst of the years make known: In wrath remember mercy (Hab 3:2) KJV We always hear good and bad news alike which we cannot deny them as facts. Some of the bad news are the failures of things we did not do right and attributed to that effect. Which we always don't want to hear them. And the good news are the success stories we hear from people, see from people, and discuss about people.

You see, nothing on this earth is so challenging than seeing that our expectations are met. So success comes as a result of learning our lessons from good and bad experiences and circumstances around us. As faith comes by hearing good and bad news not necessarily that we must build our faith in our failures but strive hard to listen to the stories and read about the successful people and emulate their good legacies, their philosophical ideas, to put them into practice. As a process of learning to develop our mental sphere. In order to develop a positive attitude to succeed, let us read the book of (Romans chapter 10:17) KJV "So then faith cometh by hearing, and hearing by the word of God. If by listening and hearing from the successful men and women created in the image and the likeness of God, can lead to success, or failures in our lives.

Then why is that we don't want to believe in the true word of God that is the light and the lamp of our path to succeed? To set some few biblical examples to support my point of view to the people of Israel, when the Prophet Elisha, prophesied about the good days ahead when there was drought in the land for a long time.

"Then Elisha said, hear ye the word of the Lord: Thus saith the Lord, tomorrow about this time shall a measure of fine flour be sold for a shekel, and two measures of barley for a shekel, in the gate of Samaria.

Then a Lord on whose hand the King leaned answered the man of God, and said. Behold, if the Lord would make windows of heaven, might this thing be?

And he said, Behold, thou shalt see it with thine eyes but shalt not cat thereof. (2 Kgs 7:1-2) KJV. Here, the following passage demonstrates all of the five human senses and to the obedient one's they were blessed according to the word of the prophet. But to the disobedient one's they though, saw the good days as prophesied by the prophet but did not enjoy the good days ahead.

The story backed the days of Elijah, the prophet with his encounter with King Ahab for turning the heart of the people to follow idolatry worship to Baalism. And Israel was led into captivity of the Syrians, besieging Samaria, to the time of Elisha, Elijah's predecessor who prophesied of an abundance of food supply supernaturally by God the next day, within the period of twenty four hours. But a man on whose hand the King leaned. Said, how could this miracle happened? In a form of disbelieve.

And Elisha, said, thou shalt see it with thine eyes, but shalt not eat thereof.

The prophecy had been made earlier by a man of God, Elijah, for the doom of Israel. And this time a man of God, by named Elisha, prophesied of abundance. There wasn't any contradiction to that effect.

This prophecy was made in the days of Elisha was fulfilled in (2 Kings chapter 7:3) KJV.

"And there were four leprous men at the entering in of the gate: and they said one to another why sit we here until we die?

Vrs 4    If we say, we will enter into the city, then the famine is in the city, and we shall die there: and if we sit still here, we die also. Now therefore come, and let us fall unto the host of the Syrians: If they save us alive, we shall live: and if they kill us, we shall but die.

Vrs 5    And they rose up in the twilight, to go unto the camp of the Syrians: and when they were come to the uttermost part of the camp of Syria, behold, there was no man there.

Vrs 6    For the Lord had made the host of the Syrians to hear a noise of chariots, and a noise of horses, even the noise of a great host: and they said one to another, lo, the King of Israel hath hired against us the Kings of the Hittites, and the Kings of Egyptians, to come upon us.

Vrs 7    Wherefore they arose and fled in the twilight, and left their tents, and their horses, and their asses, even the camp as it was, and fled for their life

Vrs 8    And when these lepers came to the uttermost part of the camp, they went into one tent, and did eat and drink, and carried thence silver, and gold, and raiment, and went and hid it, and came again, and entered into another tent, and carried thence also, and went and hid it. Isn't it very wonderful as precisely what the prophet Elisha prophesied?

And the King appointed the Lord on whose hand he leaned to have the charge of the gate and the people trode upon him in the gate, and he died as the man of God had said who spake when the king came down to him." (2 Kgs 7:17) KJV. The lepers were not selfish to disclose the good news to their fellow brothers to join them for the plunder of the Syrians. Food, clothings silver and gold were in abundance. The same man who did not believe in what the prophet said, died without enjoying the good days of the Samarians. Oh! How are the mighty falling for their disbelief? So, good and bad news comes by hearing, and what we believe has an effect over our lives.

The bible says, if ye be willing and obedient, ye shall eat the good of the land: But if ye refuse and rebel, ye shall be devoured with the sword: for the mouth of the Lord hath spoken it" (Ish 1:18-19) KJV

I believe that it is never too late for us to develop our potential.

Therefore, let the wise man listen and add knowledge to their learning.

If we don't hear and listen to the circumstances around us how could we escape the dangers ahead. That is the essence of hearing good and bad news in our daily lives.

When Adam and Eve heard the voice of the Lord God walking in the garden of Eden in the cool of the day, they hid themselves from the presence of the Lord God. Because they discovered that they were heading towards God's pronouncement of judgment for their disobedience to eat of the forbidden fruit. This is a very good example of the sense of hearing.

And the Lord God called unto Adam, and said unto him, where are thou?

And he said, I heard thy voice in the garden, and I was afraid, because I was naked: and I hid myself. And he said, who told thee that thou wast naked? Hast thou eaten of the tree whereof I commanded thee that thou shouldest not eat? (Gen 3:9-11) KJV.

We must therefore be careful for the things we hear about. Whether, it was a good or bad news they aid us to develop or deviate from our carrier goals.

# CHAPTER THREE

# The Sense of Tasting Success

Good rich meals are prepared and eaten on occasions like X'mas days, or paydays. Where people tend to forget of the bad old days behind when things were not right without counting the costs involved for what we eat or drink. Just think about the day you had nothing in your pocket for your family members to even feed on one square meal.

How does it look like? Seeing your kids weeping for the food to eat for the day as they are gathered on the dinning table expecting a breakfast, lunch or a dinner.

At certain times in your hard times though, your wife prepares food and put it on the dinning table, you ate alright but you sensed that the food tasted bitter. Why?

Because you did not enjoy the good taste you were expecting because of poverty. And at times in your good days you ate very rich delicious meals that was affordable like three to four square meals a day. The picture illustrated above can best explain and understood how a sense of taste is likened to.

I am strongly optimistic and with the opinion that after tasting the good things in life, nobody would ever like to taste bitter things again. As we always like to drink or take the bitter medicines first before we take the sweet medications at the latter. No matter what we are made of life is full of sweetness, and bitterness alike. They are bound to happen inevitably there's nothing to prevent them. But they come as a challenge to prove us to sit up and face the challenges. And that is the time we have to use our potential to niche and develop ideas with the (I.Q) intelligent quotient, to know what Gods will is for us.

Let us come to the story of Isaac and his two sons. Esau and Jacob, to explain this sense. The Bible says, when Isaac was advanced in years he had wanted to pass his legacy to Esau, his elderly son.

But something unexpected transpired with the sense of "taste", "smell", and "touch".

Isaac deliberately wanted Esau, to succeed him for his meritorious services rendered to him for years. But it wasn't so to Jacob because he was a deceiver and must learn his lesson from a dint of hard work of honesty to develop his potential rather than thinking that he was smarter than his brother Esau.

Let me repeat the story once again from the context of the Bible.

"And it came to pass, that when Isaac was old, and his eyes were dim, so that he could not see, he called Esau his eldest son, and said unto him, my son: and he said unto him, Behold, here am I, And he said, Behold now, I am old, I know not the day of my death: Now therefore take, I pray thee thy weapons, thy quiver and thy bow, and go out to the field, and take me some venison:

And make me savoury meat, such as I love, and bring it to me, that I may eat: that my soul may bless thee before I die". (Gen 27:1-4) KJV.

Vrs 5    "And Rebekah heard when Isaac spake to Esau his son: And Esau went to the field to hunt for venison, and to bring it.

Vrs 6    And Rebekah spake unto Jacob her son. Saying, Behold, I heard thy father speak unto Esau thy brother, saying.

Vrs 7    Bring me venison, and make me savoury meat, that I may eat, and bless thee before the Lord, before my death.

You see, nobody should determine of our life success journey for us except God who determines of future. How could Rebekah do such a thing by playing favoritism role for some of her kids to succeed or suffer?

As we continue the story.

Vrs 9  Go now to the flock, and fetch me from thence two good kids of the goats; and I will make them savoury meat for thy father, such as he loveth,

Vrs 10  And thou shalt bring it to thy father, that he may eat, and that he may bless thee before his death.

You see, most good parents always loved to <u>see</u> that their children succeed in life before their death. But some of the bad one's would always want their children to suffer because of parental favoritism they show to some of their kids to fail in life. Anyway, they are our parents and they can best explain and account to God on the judgment day.

So both senses of hearing and smelling are closely related to both chapters three, and four.

Therefore we develop our ideas from hearing the word of God as our number one priority, and philosophical ideas as our secondly ideas.

"So as human beings of God, s creative agents, we must emulate God, s example to display the sense of taste for the power of positive confession.

Because God used the "power of speech" to create the universe, and the "power of touch ",to form man in his image and after his likeness.

So in combination of these two senses, the universe existed. The "taste sense "here, represents the power of speech. (The tongue) which was displayed in the creational stage, when God said, "let us make man in our image and after our likeness to rule the earth and have dominion. (Gen.1:26-30.)

So the confession came as a result of the power of the tongue tamed as the (power of positive confession).

It was God's spoken word. (RHEMA).

Since the tongue is a spark of fire as stated in the book of ( proverbs chap.18:21) "Death and life are in the power of the tongue, and they that love it shall eat the fruit thereof. "(KJV. )

* Therefore, man's greatness and achievements comes as a result of innate qualities God placed in man to rule and have dominion and be fruitful, succeed and to be blessed through the power of his mouth piece with the "sense of taste ".

* There was a boy in the bible called Jabez, this boy was born honorable but was unfortunately cursed by his mother due to the hard times surrounded to his birth.

  Why would his own mother pronounce such a curse on him.? Just because of the hard times the mother went through. I don't believe that the mother would deliberately do such a thing to her own child. But just because she was under duress for the circumstances associated to the boy's birth which prompted her to do that unintentionally.

  But before the mother could realize the harm she might have caused to the boy, but it was too late to resend to the curse.

* So people should exercise constraint in their anger. In order not to commit evil by pronouncing negative speeches to our fellow human beings created in God's image.

* When the boy Jabez, grew up called on the God of Israel when he saw that his lifestyle was abnormal, .Saying, oh that thou wouldest bless me indeed, and enlarge my coast, and that thine hand might be with me, and that thou wouldest keep me from evil, that it may not grieve me: And God granted him that which he requested. ( 1 Chronicles 4: 9-10 .) Kjv.

* Jabez, saw the need to bless himself from parental curses pronounced against him because blessings and curses comes from the power of the tongue. .

  The reason been that the power of the tongue is so powerful because God demonstrated this sense to command the existence of the universe.

* And for some other reasons are that, only the sense of taste have many receptors. Due to the different taste receptors.

(I.e.)sweet -salty -bitter -umami, which detects amino acid glutamate taste found in meat, and artificial flavoring.

* The tongue is a spark of fire. So people should control their tongues to bless but not curse our fellow human beings created in the image of God. (James 3:5-8.)Kjv.
* This is the very reason why great thinkers (philosophers) don't talk a lot about unproductive things that doesn't edify. Because people gains respect and disrespect from their speeches and they are ensnared by the choice of words they use.

Have you therefore considered why you have many enemies around you?

We don't beg for respect it is reciprocal .So please people must respect themselves in their speeches for others to respect them.

* So is how Esau changed his destiny when he realized the dangers ahead of him for losing everything he had toiled for his brother Jacob due to his mother's favoritism role she played to impersonate him.

Determined not to lose sight of what his father Isaac had told him.

* "Behold, I have made him (Jacob ) thy lord, and all his brethren have I given to him for servant : and with corn and wine have I sustained him: and what shall I do now unto thee, my son.?
* And Esau said unto his father, hast thou but one blessing, my father. Bless me, even me also, O my father, And Esau lifted up his voice, and wept.
* And Isaac his father answered and said unto him, Behold, thy dwelling shall be the fatness of the earth, and of the dew of heaven from above.
* And by thy sword shalt thou live,and shalt serve thy brother, (Jacob) and it shall come to pass when thou shalt have the

dominion, that thou shalt break his joke from off thy neck. (Genesis 27:37-40.) Kjv."

* So is how Esau was challenged and rose from the life of mediocrity to the higher heights through the words of his father which echoed through his spirit.

* In this world, s life journey, people don't need to be informed of a change because of the things around us..

And the challenges people goes through are all instruments for a change. In order for people to move from pragmatic approach to confront challenges through the conventional attitude.

* Esau saw that the power of the tongue is so powerful in order to prepare himself to have broken his brother's yoke from his neck, as a result of "positive confession ".

Once has God spoken, twice have we heard them, power belongs to the Lord. Hallelujah

So as human beings, we are God's instruments for change. Therefore, we shouldn't be limited to negative thoughts because we have the power to pronounce positive things in our lives.

We shouldn't forget of the fact that both positive and negative confessions are on the power of the tongue.

* This is the reason why God asked Ezekiel about the dried bones survival and Ezekiel said, Oh Sovereign lord thou knowest. And the Lord charged Ezekiel to prophesy unto the dried, and the hopeless bones to come back to life. (Ezekiel 37:1-4.)Kjv.

So let us stop envying one another but rather promote good things and eschew evil as Rebecca did to Esau her own son. Because righteousness exalts a nation but sin is a reproach to mankind.

# CHAPTER FOUR

# The Sense of Smelling Success

How can people smell success, or does it make any sense for people to smell success? Yes, the story stated below displayed this sense in the life of Isaac. To precisely know that he was consenting his blessing upon his right son after his heart, Esau.

Yet he was obliged to do so because it was divinely orchestrated. Not only did he display this sense but was in combination with the other sense of touch, as well.

As we can read the story from Genesis, chapter (27:11-29) KJV. "And Jacob said to Rebekah, his mother, behold, Esau my brother is a hairly man, and I am a smooth man.

Vrs 12   My father peradventure will feel me, and I shall seem to him as a deceiver, and I shall bring a curse upon me, and not a blessing. The verse eleven and twelve, was the communication which transpired between Jacob, and his mother Rebekah. And the verse twenty one, reads:
And Isaac said unto Jacob, come near, I pray thee, that I may feel thee, my son, whether, thou be my very son Esau or not.

Vrs 22   And Jacob went near unto Isaac his father and he felt him, and said. The voice is Jacob's voice, but the hands are the hands of Esau. Because the sense's of touch, and smell were displayed. Isaac precisely knew that he was not speaking to the right son, Esau.

But what could he do when Jacob had justified his inclusion of getting all the qualities his brother Esau has. The evil that men do lives after them.

**Vrs 23** And he discerned him not, because his hands were hairly, as his brother Esau's hands. So he blessed him.

**Vrs 24** And he said, art thou my very son Esau? And he said, I am. We must not forget of the fact that we can impersonate people's life styles, habits and their ways of doing things to forge our ways through. But one day we shall stand before the judge of our souls to give an accountability to him. For our actions and inactions.

**Vrs 25** And he said, bring it near to me, and I will eat of my son's venison, that my soul may bless thee, And he brought it near to him, and he did eat: and he brought him wine, and he drank.

**Vrs 26** And his father Isaac said unto him, Come near now, and <u>kiss</u> me my son.

**Vrs 27** And he came near, and kiss him: and he smelled the <u>smell</u> of his raiment, and blessed him, and said, <u>see</u> the smell of my son is as the smell of the field which the Lord hath blessed:

**Vrs 28** Therefore, God give thee of the dew of heaven, and the fatness of the earth, and plenty of corn and wine.
How do you feel cheat on someone? Hmm!

**Vrs 29** Let people serve thee, and nations bow down to thee: be Lord over thy brethren, and let thy mother's sons bow down to thee: cursed be every one that curseth thee: and blessed be he that blesseth thee.
The underlined words in the phrase are contributing factors to all of the five senses that could be applied for our success or failures in life.

The tongue is a powerful weapon to bless or to destroy people created in the image and the likeness of God to bless people rather than to curse people. Because the people we bless, God will surely bless them, and those that we curse God will curse them as well.

Therefore, let us continually use the power of the tongue in a positive way to bless people. More especially, our kids, family members, friends our leaders, our nations, and even our worst enemies. For we don't know those whom the Lord has blessed.

In Genesis chapter twelve verse two, reads And I will make of thee a great nation, and I will bless thee, and make thy name great, and thou shalt be a blessing.

Vrs 3    And I will bless them that bless thee, and curse him that curseth thee: and in thee shall all families of the earth be blessed.

In the book of James chapter three verse two reads, "For in many things we offend all, if any man offend not in word, the same is a perfect man, and able also to bridle the whole body.

Vrs 3    Behold, we put bits in the horses mouths that they may obey us: and we turn about their whole body.

Vrs 4    Behold also the ships, which though they be so great, and are driven of fierce winds, yet are they turned about with a very small helm, whitersoever the governor listeth.

Vrs 5    Even so the tongue is a little member, and boasteth great things, Behold, how great a matter a little fire kindleth.

Vrs 6    And the tongue is a fire, a world of iniquity: So is the tongue among our members, that it defileth the whole body, and setteth on fire the course of nature : and it is set on fire of hell.

Vrs 7    For every kind of beasts, and of birds, and of serpents, and of things in the sea, is tamed, and hath been tamed of mankind.

Vrs 8    But the tongue can no man tame; it is an unruly evil, full of deadly poison.

Vrs 9    Therewith bless we God, even the father, and therewith curse we men, which are made after the similitude of God.

Vrs 10   Out of the same mouth proceedeth blessing and cursing. My brethren, these things ought not so to be (James 3: 2--10) KJV. It is my fervent prayer that God in his infinite power use this book to bless people to succeed in every sphere of their life. As they get a copy to read, meditate on it, and share their experience with others, to utilise their God's given talents to bless other people as well.

"It is not only that delicious foods are tasty during occasions as stated earlier when I was illustrating the "sense of taste ".

You can also believe with me that one cannot taste good or bad food or medications without a "sense of smell ".You see how the bodily parts work together as a team. ?

"Smelling (smell )- Another of the sensors that works off of a chemical reaction.

This sense combines with "taste to produce flavors for what we eat or drink. So to continue with the story,

Isaac psychologically invited Jacob to come closer to him to smell his body odor to make sure that it was Esau he was about to bless.

The story goes on to read that:

"And his father Isaac said unto Jacob, come near, I pray thee, that I may feel thee, my son, whether thou be my very son Esau or not.

And Jacob went near unto Isaac his father, and he felt him, and said, the voice is Jacob's voice, but the hands are the hands of Esau.

This is mischievous, how did he (Isaac),feel him(Jacob ?.) Because he was a hairy man. An impersonation.

And he discern him not, because his hands were hairy, as his brother Esau's hands. So he blessed him."(Gen.27:21-23)KJV.

The point I want to emphasize here is that, we can "smell success if only we have the desire for it. So don't tell me that the blind people don't have feelings to hurt them.

Are they not our fellow human beings to have neglected them from our social activities, instead of involving them.

I give credit to most of the national leaders more especially, the advanced countries like America, and FIFA, for the special accommodation and platforms they give to our fellow physically challenged and impaired brothers and sisters .

It is my desire and prayer that the whole world will copy this good habit from Americans .God bless American s and their leaders.

Why would Isaac have known that Esau was a hairy man.? Because the blind are human beings as we are.

They are God's properties so please don't cheat them or infringe on their birth rights.

We must show them some love in order for them to develop their gifts and talents. By so doing shall they be able to bring the best out of them.

# CHAPTER FIVE

# The Sense of Touching Success

As human beings the eyes is always never satisfied of the things we see or watch at around us. And they becomes a prey to tempt us as the saying "Curiosity kills the cat"

In Genesis, of the Bible when God placed Adam, and Eve, in the Garden of Eden, and warned them of the forbidden tree of life, and death. We saw that man was tempted beyond his control to look at the tree, touch it, and tasted it. So our evil desires are conceived by our lustful nature that becomes a thought or a habit to lead us into temptations. (Genesis chapter two)

Vrs 15    And the Lord God took the man, and put him into the garden of Eden to dress it and to keep it.

Vrs 16    And the Lord God commanded the man saying, of every tree of the garden thou mayest freely eat.

Vrs 17KJV    But of the tree of the knowledge of good and evil, thou shalt not eat of it: for in the day that thou eatest thereof thou shalt surely die.

In Genesis chapter three verse one) KJV.

"Now the serpent was more subtile than any beast of the field which the Lord God had made. And he said unto the woman. (woe unto man) yeah, hath God said, ye shall not eat of every tree of the garden?

Vrs 2    And the woman said unto the serpent, we may eat of the fruit of the tree of the garden;

| | |
|---|---|
| <u>Vrs 3</u> | But of the fruit of the tree which is in the midst of the garden, God hath said, ye shall not eat of it, neither shall ye <u>touch</u> it, lest ye die. |
| <u>Vrs 4</u> | And the serpent said unto the woman, ye shall not surely die: |
| <u>Vrs 5</u> | For God doth know that in the day ye eat thereof, then your eyes shall be opened, and ye shall be as god's knowing good and evil. |
| <u>Vrs 6</u> | And when the woman saw that the tree was good for food, and that it was pleasant to the eyes, and a tree to be desired to make one wise, she took of the fruit thereof, and did eat, and gave also unto her husband with her, and he did eat. |
| <u>Vrs 7</u> | And the <u>eyes</u> of them both were opened, and they knew that they were naked, and they sewed fig leaves together and made themselves aprons. |
| <u>Vrs 8</u> | And they <u>heard</u> the voice of the Lord God walking in the garden in the cool of the day: And Adam and his wife hid themselves from the presence of the Lord God amongst the trees of the garden. |
| <u>Vrs 9</u> | And the Lord God called unto Adam, and said unto him, where are thou? |
| <u>Vrs 10</u> | And he said, I <u>heard</u> thy voice in the garden, and I was afraid, because I was naked, and I hid myself. |
| <u>Vrs 11</u> | And he said, who told thee that thou wast naked? Hast thou eaten of the tree, whereof. I commanded thee that thou shouldest not eat? |
| <u>Vrs 12</u> | And the man said, the woman whom thou gavest to be with me, she gave me of the tree, and I did eat. |

You see, here that Adam was trying to justify himself and accused God for giving him a partner. And that is how human beings are always apt to doing. We don't want to accept blames been shift to us by our bosses at the work place for fearing that we may be fired. A simple I am sorry from husbands and wives, could have saved some marriages but each person is a boss unto him or herself. May God have mercy on us.

Vrs 13      And the Lord God said unto the woman, what is this that thou hast done? And the woman said, the serpent beguiled me, and I did eat.

You see, the struggle continues unabated. Here and there because of I am sorry. Because the serpent could not speak, it could also might have said, Lord, because you threw me out of your presence as an angle, I could no way come back to inherit my position anymore, I decided to also create confusion for man to lose his position of trust.

Vrs 14      And the Lord God said unto the serpent, because thou hast done this, thou art cursed above all cattle, and above every beast of the field: Upon thy belly shalt thou go, and dust shalt thou eat all the days of thy life.

God could have destroyed the serpent, but spared it for some reasons that one day, he might display his power and might to proof to the devil that he God, is in control of the universe.

God sparing the serpent depicts that man will be an enemy to the serpent in our daily life to proof that all the circumstances that man faces, will lead man to be a dependent of God to bring creativity.

That is the reason why man has always, and will always face a life struggles to depend on God for solutions to his problem.

Vrs 15    And I will put enemity between thee and the woman, and between thy seed and her seed, it shall bruise thy head, and thou shalt bruise his heel.

Vrs 16    And unto the woman he said, I will greatly multiply thy sorrow and thy conception: In sorrow thou shalt bring forth children: and thy desire shall be to thy husband, and he shall rule over thee.

Vrs 17    And unto Adam he said, because thou hast hearkened unto the voice of thy wife, and hast eaten of the tree, of which I commanded thee saying. Thou shalt not eat of it: Cursed is the ground for thy sake : in sorrow shalt thou eat of it, all the days of thy life

Vrs 18    Thorns also and thistles shall it bring forth to thee: and thou shalt eat the herb of the field.

Vrs 19    In the sweat of thy face shalt thou eat bread, till thou return unto the ground : for out of it wast thou taken : for dust thou art, and unto dust shalt thou return.

Vrs 20    And Adam called his wife's name Eve: because she was the mother of all living.

Vrs 21    Unto Adam also and to his wife did the Lord God make coats of skins and clothed them.

Vrs 22    And the Lord God said, behold, the man is become as one of us, to know good and evil, and now, lest he put forth his <u>hand</u> and take also of the tree of life, and eat, and live forever.

Vrs 23(KJV)    Therefore the Lord God sent him forth from the garden of Eden, to till the ground from whence he was taken.

Vrs 24 (KJV)   So he drove out the man: and he placed at the east of the garden of Eden cherubims, and a flaming sword which turned every way, to keep the way of the tree of life.

Hmmm!!! So, does that mean God didn't want man to know good, and evil? Lest man put forth his hand to touch of the tree of life, to eat and live forever? These are some of the challenging questions to provoke man to create wealth as God's agents of creativity. Therefore, who is man that God is mindful of, though, we were made little lower than angels, God did not entrust the earthly things to them. So the question of the distance from between God's position to angels, to that of man, depicts of the distance of heaven to the earth.

And the height of man to God, is the length of time and space we human beings can develop, create, and recreate.

In the book of Psalms chapter eight verse one reads "O Lord our Lord, how excellent is thy name in all the earth! Who hast set thy glory above the heavens.

Vrs 2   Out of the mouth of babes and sucklings hast thou ordained strength because of thine enemies, that thou mightest still the enemy and the avenger.

Vrs 3   When I consider thy heavens, the works of thy fingers, the moon and the stars, which thou hast ordained.

Vrs 4   What is man, that thou art mindful of him? and the son of man, that thou visitest him.?

Vrs 5   For thou hast made him a little lower than the angels, and hast crowned him with glory and honour.

Vrs 6 KJV.   Thou madest him to have dominion over the works of thy hands : thou hast put all things under his feet.

| | |
|---|---|
| <u>Vrs 7</u> | All sheep and oxen, yea, and the beasts of the field. |
| <u>Vrs 8</u> | The foul of the air, and the fish of the sea, and whatsoever passeth through the paths of the sea's. |
| <u>Vrs 9 (KJV)</u> | O Lord our Lord, how excellent is thy name in all the earth. |
| | The illustrated chart of wisdom displayed below can best explain the position of God, the angels, and the position of man on earth. |

→ Notes to understand God's administrative set up and God's position occupied.
→ In relations with Angels.
→ And to that of man's position.

- The height from man to Angels.
- And the height from man to God.
- The answer equals to how tall is man's success?

→ creativity.
→ innovations.
→ inventions.
→ Re-discoveries.

Is it not a sad story that man was expelled from his estate of dignity, position of trust to start a new life, to inherit God's curse? The glory of God was no more a shadow to protect Adam and Eve than to be cast away from God's bounty provision of supply to poverty, sickness, nakedness, and affliction. The story illustrated above means that God was therefore testing man to use his creative ability to know his position by the height that he can travel to plan about things in life.

I thank God that from the scriptures we just read, explained that the sense of <u>touch</u> could bring a lot of illuminations to demonstrate over one thousand sermons and lessons to learn from.

Since this book is not a product of man's wisdom rather, God's inspired revelation by his spirit to his servant. The sense of touch, as the last chapter of the write up, there are certain things we are not allowed to touch or taste because they are disobedience to God's commandments.

In Genesis chapter two verse seventeen, "But of the tree of the knowledge of good and of evil, thou shall not eat of it.

Today, the world want to know everything because of advancement in technology, a high rate of researches are made within the clock to bring man back to his occupied position again. Through inventions and innovations, to rediscover things that are not permitted to be searchable and that is the tree of the knowledge of good and evil. It is good as God's agents of creativity but the world today must be very careful for where God had placed his dissatisfaction stamp of approval we are not to touch those things to provoke God to anger. Even though, they are signs of development of adding value to mother nature doesn't give us the impetus to research into everything.

That is the reason why even the super-power nations have today failed God by placing him outside their thinking. Though, knowledge helps us to quantify good from evil, we must be very careful in order not to add woes to our God's given peaceful atmosphere on the earth.

Because of knowledge, the eye and the ear, gate pleasure senses, are at risk of disobedience to the commandments of God.

We disobey God, and our national leaders, church leaders, because of knowledge of seeing into things, hearing about things, touching, and tasting of the forbidden fruit. Therefore, mankind is spiritually dead and this is the very reasons people cannot develop their potential.

We then turn to be God's enemies, instead of God calling us as his children and friends. I don't think that I am contradicting from this <u>sense of touch</u> but we must be mindful of the things we touch to bring blessings of God in our lives.

So I believe that by bringing all of the five senses together as God's creative agents, in an innovative ways places man in a unique position as God's representatives on earth. In order for us to deal away with traditional beliefs of theory that success is a luck from God to some few minority people on earth to enjoy God's heavenly bounties. It is a big lie.

# CHAPTER SIX

# Creative Thinking

The key to achieving individuals and organizational goals is creative thinking.

Because creative thinkers are the world's problem solvers through innovations they bring out what is inside of them. i.e. Their unborn ideas ahead of time as visioners.

This is my strongest belief and what motivated me to come out with the five Human Senses together in my own experience as a pastor. Some people think that due to their incapacitated conditions would prompt people to sympathize with them to appeal to governmental and benevolent organizations for support to meet their carrier goals and family needs.

Whiles some other people also believes that despite of their ill-health conditions they can use creative thinking to create things in the job market to survive.

I don't dispute any of the facts either that is why I am therefore using the book to appeal to people with weak consciences to eradicate this canker — of using incapacitation as an excuse to bury their God's given dreams and talents to pursue reasoning as a process of continuous thinking in a logical way. With opinion and ideas that are based on logical thinking known as creativity.

In order that people may niche ideas on their own rather than to build upon other people's experiences.

I am therefore of the view that mankind must find solutions to the world's most major crises as why on this earth only few people have had asset to God's Provision of blessings to succeed? Whiles the majority of the people are living under a closed heavens.

My question goes on this way,

- Why is it that out of 100% only 10% of the people have actually reasoned to reach the level where they occupy today?
- Why is it that the 90% princes go on foot like slaves, whiles slaves sit on horseback?
- You see, we must admit of the fact that getting reasons to problems to release our potentials is an ongoing process which doesn't culminate from the silver platter but by dint of hard work, enthusiasm and determination put together. And out of these people develop their five human senses through creative thinking in their reasoning sphere to think like the creator.

  And that is the reason why people should not give up for who and what they are made of?

  To back my point for what others have done in the past, the present, and what we can also do in the near future.

  Through reasoning the world has come out with great inventors who have manufactured automobiles as means of transportation. Airplanes, Steam Engines etc.

  Purposely to assist productions in factories and industries
- To convey people to and from their destinations all over the world and it is still ongoing.
- For Mass and Media Communication Equipment's to convey messages through the internet, radios, and other electronic machines.

  Sir, Isaac Newton's work for example represents one of the greatest contributions to science ever made by an individual. Most notably, Newton derived the Law of "Universal Gravitation" invented the branch of mathematics called calculus, and performed experiments, investigating the nature of light and color (sources of information – Encarta Encyclopedia – Rex Features.)

Now that we have understood it clearly for what others have done in the past, I believe that it is left for us to apply our five human senses through the following context, then shall we be able to understand reasoning in logical thinking. Here are some of the few questions we should ask ourselves.

Who are you (we) and why are you (we) here on this planet earth, and our role(s) to play in the global supermarket?

These questions will fire our imaginations to figure out whether things are appropriate or inappropriate as expected.

• This explosion of insight will logically show us whether we are on course to use our abilities, skills, gifts and talents and our experiences together to reason. To cause changes expected in our world today. Whether as individuals, or organizations.

In my own experience as a pastor, the modern day Christianity looks like a tradition without creative thinking amongst even the most believers of the gospel.

Thinking that the gospel is only a message of salvation and peace without also considering the other side of the gospel as a message of good things to happen.

So I have been teaching the church members always that, accepting the gospel of Jesus Christ points to us that the one side of the gospel is for peace. And the other side of the gospel also points to us as good things to happen through creativity, innovations, and to bring success. So I entreat the pastors to not only preach about prosperity to the church members but also to teach the members to come up with creative ideas out of their God's given talents. This is the greatest gift for the pastors and the intellectuals to impart in people as their way of incentive rather than doing them disincentive. For not letting them to know the truth to emancipate them from mental slavery.

I am therefore of the view that through the development of man's skills he must be <u>dependent</u> on God and other things within his reasoning sphere to bring creativity.

- Through man's level of <u>independency</u> where he must know his position of strength and importance in God's socio-economic and political programme on this earth where he can make good use of his potential.

- And through man's level of <u>inter-dependency</u> whereby, he must be able to depend on other network partners, through Technological Advancement. As far as creativity into many fields like Psychological – Sociological – Anthropological and Political are concerned.

- After man has been able to develop his mental skills through inventions he must be able to market what he has developed to other people by transforming his ideas into sale and pass it to other people of the world. (in the network-economy)

- Therefore it is time for man to structurally transform his world into a happy environment because we cannot afford to underrate the potentials in any mortal being. Because the backgrounds and the level of exposures of the individuals obviously contribute to the overall output. Which in turn affect the inventions of the things in our world today.

- It is therefore worthy of acceptance to note that people must be brought up, educated, polished and be encouraged before they would be able to effectively carry out their divine roles on earth.

- Since man is economically a viable resource you and I, as the entrepreneurs in God's business are not left out to exhibit a higher level of effective co-ordination of affairs of the resources placed in our hands to manage them.

We must realize that these resources are invaluable and their mismanagement cannot be affordable in the day of accountability of our talents before the creator.

- And finally, we cannot rate man with anything, no matter whosoever, the person is. Whether they are schooled or unschooled, whether they be knowledgeable or novice, disabled or physically impaired, they are very important and could be the most powerful tool at your disposal in this dispensation of God's socio-economic and political programme.

- For there is no human being on earth created to remain in a static state of mind.

Provided he can use his Intelligent Quotient (I.Q.) to invent in his field of choice to create events.

This is the reason why I always want to develop people to make good use of their time, in their generation through encouragement and motivation to come up with their God's given potential. I believe that this should be a general habit for all to follow to be part of the advocating team to motivate and encourage people to wake up from their slumber, especially the less privileged ones. And if you are not part of the wakeup call then there's something wrong somewhere.

Therefore it is my prayer that the good Lord – will help us to change in our thinking sphere to respect people as invaluable resource to invest in them.

I have used creative thinking in my own life experience as a tool to transform my dreams into reality right from my early childhood I grew up at age five and only saw that my father always complained of his ill-health and passed away when I had just started my primary school. In a little village from my home town the District Capital, where my parents were peasant farmers.

The three of my other siblings were left in the custody of our grandparents in the village when my mother decided to take leave to the city, our home town with a notion that she was not prepared to marry my late father's elderly brother. As she was compelled to do so by my grandparents as to be able to take a very good care of her three kids.

My eldest sister was seven years, and I was five years old, and our youngest brother was almost three years as at that time. So my mother left us behind to her own parents as a widow.

Though, it was very pathetic for her to leave us behind as a young widow who loved her kids. And my grandparents did not also allow her to take us along to the city.

And that is where really life started from. The time we needed our Daddy, and Mum, and they were not there to be by our side for comfort and parental care.

So I can say with confidence that at age five, the immediate Parental Training, Education and Development and Courtesy were in absentia. My grandparents laid little emphasis on our personal needs because of a lot of their farming activities, and the size of the family and relatives could be about almost one hundred people. In a very big house to accommodate all of us in the village. And here was the case that we had to learn to do things on our own.

And that is where really life found the three of her kids. The very moment we would have loved to be by our parents they rather deserted us without any comfort or shelter.

So their attention was divided here and there to be able to attend to our personal basic needs.

You can just imagine how life could be at that time for (100-150) people living in a compound house combined with different temperamental and attitudinal behaviors of typical villagers.

And here was the case we had to learn to do things on our own by getting up early in the mornings to go to the stream to fetch water before we got prepared to school and after school hours in the evenings every day for about three kilometers.

You can imagine that if you don't get up early on time like four o'clock in the morning you will be late to school to be punished. And you can also not get your target of the drums you are supposed to fill every day.

In fact travelling with my sister to the stream every day to fetch for water was a hell situation.

And also not only that, we have to pound "fufu" after school hours in the evenings for almost three to four hours to get our super ready to eat. You see, in Africa, almost ninety percent of the majority of the people are farmers. So farming activities was part of my training more especially during the weekends and for some of us who were living in the rural areas.

I personally didn't like the farming activities but what could I do without joining the farming activities after school hours?

In fact we were totally deprived from the basic necessities of life like good health care facility, no electricity in the village to read your books in the night, nor to even mention of ironing your school uniform.

We had to depend on lanterns in the night to read and write our school assignments of which our study time could be interrupted by someone who comes in to take the light for other purpose whiles studying.

You can imagine your attention was always divided during your homework exercise. As a matter of fact, I really didn't like to stay with my grandparents in the village because of the enslavement situation we were going through. But thank God for my life survival which is by His grace the three of us are able to succeed today.

I stayed in the village for sixteen years until after I had completed my Elementary School and left to the city to join my mother who was a very successful business woman in bakery industry.

I never gave up in life during my sixteen years stay in the village with my grandparents and as a poor boy. But rather, developed my talents as a very good footballer, a good singer at the school and church choir, comedian to entertain the villagers.

And will sometimes organize the youth after school hours for entertainment.

So at age twelve I was able to save some money out of my talent's income to buy my personal needs and that of my younger brother.

We shouldn't underestimate our gifts for with much persistence they shall open a way for us and usher us unto high places.

I left the village and came to the city to continue with my education and took interest in football which landed me to play for my school team and also registered in the Second-Division league with the "Young Hearts of Oak" at Wenchi, in the Brong Ahafo Region of Ghana.

I decided not to play the football again due to its association in ritualism and occultic activities involved as at those days. Morcover, my spirit was in pursuit of seeking the Lord but did not know the way to go.

Initially, I didn't understand the life I was going through because I was earning some money for the football I was playing. And all of a sudden decided not to play again.

I now can understand it better that God was giving me a life experience to go through in order to educate people to bring their life dreams into reality.

And out of creativity, innovations and inventions to re-discover their talents from their five human senses as well.

Because success is an achievement of one's goals. To conclude with my life story encounter with the Lord, my Christian experience started from my early childhood as a church goer and a chorister but did not have a personal encounter with the Lord. Because my grandparents were not staunch Christians to emulate their Christian life but were mere church goers. More especially, my grandmother who was a traditionalist practicing herbal medicines to mid-wifery in the village. A church goer who could not even tell you who Jesus was.

So my conversion into Christianity encounter started during my first job with the Volta – River Authority (V.R.A) at the Bui-Dam Camp in the Brong Ahafo Region of Ghana, in 1978.

Where I was working as a machine operator and a mechanic during one of my normal routing duties as engine attendant around the mid-night of about 1.30 am. I fell in a trance and saw Jesus who invited me to a very big and empty church building.

And He put a robe on me and asked me to stretch forth my hands towards the empty pews. And as I did that to my surprise, I saw that the empty pews were immediately filled to capacity with a lot of people. He then led me in the spirit to the people though there was no life in them on the pews, and He asked me to stretch forth my hands again towards the dead bodies. I saw that the dead bodies were all raised back to life again. He then asked me to open my mouth wide to anoint with oil.

And after anointing my mouth with some oil, I saw some flames of fire coming out of my mouth when I was asked to utter some words in a form of preaching.

He then asked me to look up to the sky and saw an inscription of "The Second Coming of Christ, and "Behold He Cometh with Clouds: And every eye shall see Him, and they also which pierced Him: And all kindred's of the earth shall wail because of Him, even so Amen" (Rev. 1:7) KJV.

The words were boldly written for people to see it.

And as He showed me a lot of eschatological events that shall culminate to His coming, I started panicking. And He told me not to panic because He's in charge of the events shown to me to be a witness unto people of the world.

That He had delivered me from my sin to be able to turn the hearts of people to repentance to God and have faith in Him.

He reminded me to take note of all the things shown to me and write about the events in the future. He then waved me and left the scene and when I came to my senses I saw that it was a vision. Not really knowing that Jesus was calling me to ministry and to preach about the things He showed me. Yet still, I never gave my life to Him as at that time and as a young man who was receiving attractive salary to pursue my youthful desires. In fact this Call of God in my life kept on to hunt me after seven years later until I finally gave my life to Jesus Christ as my personal Lord and Savior. That was in the year 1984, when Jesus Christ took full control of my entire life.

I then took personal interest to go to the Bible College in the year (1988-1990) in my own church Bible School to study Theology in Biblical Studies.

And officially started my pastoral duties from 1990, up to date without any regret for the Call of God in my life and to the life of others. As far as creativity and innovations are concerned to proof my ministry for the past 26 years' experience in Preaching – Teaching – Counseling and writing of Religious books to the glory of God. And the Lord is faithful to his Covenant Promises He made with me since that trance encounter in (1977) at Bui-Dam Camp. So at times when I minister to people and more especially those who came to me for prayer and counseling? I realized that most of the problems they encountered were not directly associated with demonic forces but as a result of lack of knowledge and understanding to natural things people perish. They make demons very popular for their inability to perform certain tasks – within their control through creative thinking to rediscover their potential.

Let me narrate a story when God visited me in 1977, to confirm the covenant He made with me in one of the Local Assemblies I was pastoring at Effiekuma, in the Western Region of Ghana.

It was in a form of "DOVE" visitation which came to me in the newly mission house I had built and moved in for 30 days. You will be surprised to believe that the "DOVE" brought a lot of blessing to my family and the church members.

And in the year 2016, I had another "Dove" visitation encounter in my new house at Kumasi, in Ghana, after I had left to the United States with my wife.

My daughter who was left behind called us one day and said, Daddy, you got another visitor in the house and asked her who that visitor was?

And my daughter told me that there was another "Dove" visitation and even posted the picture of the "DOVE" to me in my what's up for us to believe. I called her back home and told her that our God is a covenant renewer of His promises to us and is still confirming His Covenant with my family even in our absence from home. Praise God Almighty.

To confirm this I have even decided to print the picture of the "DOVE" in my upcoming book very soon to bring comfort and a lot of blessing and inspiration into your home as you lay hold your hands on the book. And the five senses success as well to see that in our desperate needs God is always present to bring things under control. May God of Abraham, Isaac and Jacob richly bless you! As you become part and parcel of this ministry of support to reach others who are suffering.

To release your potential to create wealth, riches and honor. And as you endeavor to support the angels by your good deeds, and as the redeemed of the lord Amen!

# CONCLUSION

Today, the highlighted stories of the world's most successful men and women to motivate and rejuvenate our lives are pivoted from the various fields through innovative skills and good sense of judgment needs to be desired.

- The music industry.
- The sports industry
- The entertainment industry.

You can imagine that without a good sense of judgment people are not going to be creative and nothing happens in terms of the above mentioned industries. And this places man in a void position. Because of man's inability to perform his task assigned to him on earth.

That is the reason why the generation today have good reasons to enjoy life out of people's toils and sweat. They have good legacies emulated from our predecessors not only for the areas they succeeded. But in those areas they failed in life as well.

To motivate us to overcome the challenges we face in our lives.

Here are some few people whose lives have motivated me most as my role models. His excellency, the President of the U.S.A. Mr. Barak Obama. In his address to our late president when he came to Ghana, he said, "Yes we can" still make it in Africa, if our institutions are structured and strengthened very well.

I thank God for his life and for his good leadership qualities displayed as a man of peace to promote good economic and stability measures put in place for his tenure in office, for the people of America to enjoy the riches of the land.

I also acknowledge the fact that he could not achieve this success without the good foundation laid in place by his predecessors.

Long live America, long live his excellency the President, Mr. Barak Obama.

"We the People"!

Not forgetting my spiritual fathers of the gospel and my church leaders I appreciate them so much who have brought me this far

And as the founding fathers of "Pentecostalism" in Ghana

The Christ Apostolic Church International, led by the late Apostle Peter Newman Anim.

Who passed a good legacy to the previous and the current leadership to spearhead the administrative affairs of the church in good governance of peace and tranquility. These spiritual fathers are my role models of impartation of anointing in my ministry.

The current chairman, Apostle Dr. Stephen Ntow Kwame Amoani, and his supportive team the National Executive Council members (N.E.C.) of CACINT.

The ex-chairman, Apostle Dr. Micheal Nimoh, and all of the previous leadership of this wonderful church. May God wonderfully and richly bless them all.

And to my spiritual father, Rev. Dr. Morris Cerullo, who was accredited and called by God with signs and wonders accompanying his ministry for the past sixty eight years, raised God's victories armies in the whole world to preach the gospel of our Lord Jesus Christ. In fact, he is my mentor, role model, spiritual father, and a partner in ministry.

Daddy God bless you.

So all the people mentioned in the book are few examples I could lay my hands on choosing them as role models for all of us to emulate their life styles of success

They used their God's given talents to create wealth in their generation of conquest to affect many lives. Their successes secret experience was based on dint of hard work for using their five senses as key factors.

Some of the world most successful people were women of power from philosophical and biblical point of view, who supported their men with encouragement, love and support to succeed. Therefore, my concerned is that people must be motivated by throwing our infringing support to back them to come up with innovative ideas to solve the 21st century problems facing the global world.

Because, "The height by great men reached and kept were not attained by certain flight, but they while their companions slept, were toiling upward in the night"

(Quotation by #1941 Laura Moncur's motivational quotation)
by Henry Wadsworth (long fellow) US poet (1807-1882)

So God in his infinite wisdom created man in his image and after his likeness as the Prophet Isaiah, spoke about Gods attributes in chapter fifty nine, and the book of Hebrews chapter 4:15 ("For we have not an high priest which cannot be touched with the feeling of our infirmities: but was in all points tempted like as we are, yet without sin

Vrs 16 (KJV)    Let us therefore come boldly unto the throne of grace, that we may obtain mercy, and find grace to help in time of need.

Therefore God purposely created us to be like him. So that in the absence of creation, man can also re-create, re-think, to bring innovation or add value to the five human senses.

And by so doing, we can see failure as success. This is what this book adds up to.

I therefore encourage people to buy and read this book because of its inspiration.

This book is not an excerpts from any material apart from the illustrational, introductory page of Aristotle's quotes of the five human senses I give credit to.

You may not get the information from any source of material. Glory be to God in the highest. Amen!

I am appealing to or and sundry to get a copy of this book to support this project work to help alleviate poverty for lack of creativity, there should be abundance of heavenly wisdom and understanding to bring success to people. May the good Lord help you to develop your potential as you read it. Because your attitude shall determine your altitude.

Since we have a divine being who can be touched with the feeling of our infirmities. The five human senses comes with some feelings of deficiencies to render man as weak on earthen vessels to draw near to God for solutions to his problems.

So in the absence of the aforementioned senses of: -

* Touch - To bring creation, creativity, manufacturing and production and inventions to man's daily activities, how would our world look like? ?
* Sight - In the absence of the sense of sight, how would the human body look like or relate to one another? Or respond and react to Mother Nature in terms of beauty.
* Taste - In the absence of the sense of taste, how would the food we eat and the water we drink every day taste like. ? Or to differentiate the natural and artificial flavors.
* Smell - In the absence of the sense of smell, how would our atmospheric climate condition look like? ?

Pollution and degradation everywhere for the air we breathe to cause a wide spread of diseases to affect our health and bring environmental changes.

* Hearing - In the absence of the sense of hearing, how would people react to information?? News around the world, more especially to disseminate information across the globe. So would the world - our world depict as nothing to look at, hear about, touch with, taste and smell about.

And how would people believe that there is a divine God to trust him as a creator. ?

# WISDOM MOTIVATION.

There lived two physically impaired friends in a certain village where there was a severe famine.

They decided to go to the stream to fish very far away from their village. How could they get to the stream when one was blind and the other friend was also a cripple? ?

So the blind man suggested an idea that he the blind will carry the cripple at his back whilst the cripple uses his sights to guide the way to the stream.

The idea sounds good to both of them to go to the stream and came back home safely. Their bait brought forth a lot of fish and frogs together.

When they came home to prepare soup for a dinner the cripple in his smartness separated the frog meat from the fish and placed them in front of the blind.

As they were eating the blind didn't feel very comfortable because of the frog meat stiffness. He could not chew the meat and decided to pull it out of his mouth. And very fortunately for the blind, some tip of the soup entered into his eyes which was very painful to strain his eyes . Lo, and behold, there was a miracle.

His eyes were opened and saw that he was not given the fish of his choice and therefore decided to give the cripple a chase to teach him a lesson.

When the cripple saw the danger ahead decided to run for his life. And fortunately for the cripple, and as he struggled to rise saw himself running from the blind.

So both of them saw that there had been an instant intervention of a miracle. For the cripple to walk and the blind to see. .

Now the question is who was to be blamed. ? They both agreed to come together as best friends ever had been than before.

Though the cripple was playing intelligence on the blind not knowing that in our weakness God had ordained strength.

So this is how creativity works by bringing ideas together to establish an opinion.

* Therefore this is how the five human senses works together as a team without looking down on any weak state of the other bodily parts.
* Since we are all members of the body of Christ, devoid of our various religious beliefs and political background s, we must be tolerant to one another. .
* If the foot should say, I am not of the body, is it therefore not of the body. ? Or if the ear, or the eye shall say they are not part of the body, how would the body look like. ?

Team means :.

T-- together

E-- each

A-- achieve

M-- much.

## Words of Wisdom from the Wise Man

* There is an evil I have seen under the sun, the sort of error that arises from a ruler. Fools are put in many high positions, while the rich occupy the low ones.
* I have seen slaves on horse back, while princes go on foot like slaves – Eccl 10:5-7.
* Under three things the earth trembles, under four it cannot bear up: a servant who becomes king, a fool who is full of food.

- Four things on earth are small, yet they are extremely wise: ants are creatures of little strength, yet they store up their food in the summer.
- An unloved woman who is married and a maid servant who displaces her mistress.
- Conneys are creatures of little power, yet they make their home in the crags
- Locusts have no king, yet they advance in ranks: a lizard can be caught with the hand, yet is found in Kings Palaces (Pro. 30:21-29).

So the above words of motivation will fire our imagination for man to find solution to problems as why only few people have had asset to God's provision of blessings and the majority of God's people even in the church are under closed heaven.

You may get solution to most of the world's problems in my next book.

# KEY THINKING

* You need an environment which keeps and polish the key images on which your styles are built.
* Important lessons and strategies can be learned from the behavior of others and be incorporated into your own style.
* Your natural style which is based on your own qualities must not be totally subject to any external influence.

# SUCCESSORS DECODER

The question is what's the secret of the successors. ?

And how were they able to make things happen?

And most importantly, can you do what they have done. ? "Yes we can " on quote from president Barack Obama of the United States.

* In this situation, you must succeed and be known. Otherwise you would die off gradually and be forgotten by the world around you.
  We must understand the following tips below :-
* One bit of idea must not be treated as irrelevant unless you judge it's pro's and cons, for it could be relevant to support you for the rest of your life.
* Don't always forget to back your ideas with a "plan of action "before it could be turned into a profitable venture.
* Because very few venture explorers will dare invest in your concept. Or even condescend to talk to you about, until they have reviewed your blueprint for making it happen.
* Once you have completed your vision strategies you must begin to assemble the resources needed to bring it to life.
* Understand that risk capital -skilled employee working facilities and eager volunteers are poised to help you get a piece of vast global marketplace. Where well-conceived mission ideas can produce mind-boggling results, practically overnight.
* Remember that starting any venture before the "essential pieces "are put in place is dangerous and can be hazardous to your financial -health.
* Mind you that the "essential pieces "are not necessarily a huge capital amount of money put together with furnished facilities. Rather, this could be the few hands of people needed to compliment your effort. (Take off project ).
* You need to proof to the world of investors that you are a potential winner. This would give you the enough take '-off capital
* You see, success in life comes out of good judgment and good judgment, comes from experience. And experience is born out of discerning good ideas from the bad ones.

* If your concept and mission plan are right, then successors can launch their vision in the worst possible conditions.
* If you really want to be a winning executive, you must possess the ability to overcome even the most seemingly insurmountable obstacles. Since you are bound to encounter crises and adversity to make you win or loose.
* You therefore need to develop a radical spirit to succeed because success is achieved by a fighting spirit.

# ACKNOWLEDGEMENT

- To my publishers – Xlibris
- To my Publishing Consultant, Mariel Perez.
- Who typed the manuscripts – Al Rodriguez, Kenneth Gomez
- The Printing Press – Xlibris
- Dr Edward Ade, (Rector of Oracle University (Kumasi, Ghana) for his wonderful words of wisdom).
- Mr Charles Boadi, my brother in law for his encouragement for this project work who is pursuing his Phd in Multi-Cultural Education in the U.K. with his beautiful wife Mrs. Cynthia Asabea Boadi
- And all others who helped in diverse ways to produce this book.
- And my former boss, Mr John Aidoo, who once advised me that George, don't let age be a barrier to your carrier goals.

# ABOUT THE AUTHOR

The author of "5 Human Senses Success" is Rev. George Paul Takyi, an Area Head Pastor of The Christ Apostolic Church International, who is on study leave in the United States of America. Rev. Takyi, is married to Mrs. Helena Takyi with two kids. Miss Anna Tarry Takyi, and Master Gershom Obeng Takyi.

He shares his Christian experience for the past twenty-six years as an (End Time Preacher) of the gospel in a unique way through preaching, teaching, and writing of books. To convey his messages to the world.

The Lord has used him in many areas to preach the gospel of our Lord Jesus Christ, on Eschatological Events (End Time Messages) in Burkinafaso - Cote de voire, and in both Rural and Urban Cities in Ghana, and in the United States of America, where he currently lives.

- Rev Takyi, in his academic pursuit holds Diploma in Theology in Biblical Studies of (Christ Apostolic Church International, Bible School) Kumasi-Ghana in 1988
- He holds both his Bachelor, and Master's Degree in Integrated Mission Theology, and Church Administration with (Oracle University) Santasi, - Kumasi, Ghana (2007)

# ABOUT THE BOOK

The book talks about what Rev Takyi believes that people should be allowed to develop their God's given talents, gifts, skills and competences to create wealth out of their 5 Human Senses to Succeed in this world life journey to be self-supporting.

## His Mission Statement

Is to solicit for financial assistance from benevolent organizations to support this project work. In order to reach the poor and the needy ones. More especially, the underprivileged people in the Rural Communities in Africa, and the world a large and this is what Rev. Takyi, stands for.

CPSIA information can be obtained
at www.ICGtesting.com
Printed in the USA
BVHW041437030619
550011BV00012B/649/P

9 781733 055871